SHOWIN

PRICE STERN SLOAN

PRICE STERN SLOAN LIMITED, NORTHAMPTON, ENGLAND

It was a very hot day in the land of Do-As-You're-Told. In fact, it was the hottest day that anyone could remember.

Tidyup decided to call on his friend Clean-Your-Teeth for a dip in his swimming pool.

Stoppit, of course, went too.

They found Clean-Your-Teeth taking it easy by the side of the pool.

He was pleased to see them.
He could show them his latest dive.

Tidyup thought that was a good idea. He was always impressed by Clean-Your-Teeth.

Stoppit wasn't. He thought he was just a big show off.

Clean-Your-Teeth jumped on the diving board and did a really splendid dive.

He was a very good swimmer too. But he didn't feel like swimming, so – click! – he snapped his fingers and an air bed appeared. How clever!

Stoppit didn't think so though.

Then it was Tidyup's turn. He took a great big jump from the side.

And all the water splashed out of the pool!

Stoppit thought that was funny.

Until Clean-Your-Teeth snapped his
fingers and a hose appeared in
Stoppit's hand!

It didn't take Stoppit long to fill the pool again. Then, guess what?

He turned the hose on the others!

Clean-Your-Teeth decided something must be done to keep Stoppit out of mischief. He snapped his fingers.

Click! A sandpit appeared. They thought it would be fun to build sandcastles.

Stoppit and Tidyup's sandcastles
were very nice.

Clean-Your-Teeth's were fantastic!

Stoppit didn't like that.

In fact, he lost his temper.

Tidyup had to give him a good bounce to calm him down. That always did the trick.

Now, without realising it, Tidyup and Stoppit had stepped on to the diving board.

Stoppit was being bounced higher and higher into the air. Suddenly . . .

Oh, what a dive! Three backward somersaults and a twist! Clean-Your-Teeth was impressed. He snapped his fingers.

Click. Click. Click!